Not
Quite
What I Was
Planning

2012.
Knowing Michael
made my life richer.
(Happy 75th!)

Nina

Not Quite What I Was Planning

Six-Word Memoirs
by Writers Famous and Obscure

From SMITH Magazine

Edited by
RACHEL FERSHLEISER
and LARRY SMITH

HARPER

An Imprint of HarperCollins*Publishers*
www.harpercollins.com

The editors would like to thank SMITH Magazine cofounder Tim Barkow, who was there from word one; Twitter, which helped spread the word fast and far; and the thousands of brillant memoirists who shared the words in the first place.

Share your six-word story at sixwordmemoir.com or any story at SMITH Magazine, smithmag.net.

All photographs and illustrations are courtesy of the contributors unless otherwise noted.

Photograph on page ii courtesy of Justin Dodd.

HarperCollins books may be purchased for educational, business, or sales promotional use. For information please write: Special Markets Department, HarperCollins Publishers, 10 East 53rd Street, New York, NY 10022.

A paperback edition of this book was published in 2008 by Harper Perennial, an imprint of HarperCollins Publishers.

Designed by Justin Dodd

Library of Congress Cataloging-in-Publication Data is available upon request.

ISBN 978-0-06-171371-2

10 11 12 ID/RRD 10 9 8 7 6 5 4

Introduction

LEGEND HAS IT THAT ERNEST HEMINGWAY WAS ONCE challenged to write a story in six words. Papa came back swinging with, **"For sale: baby shoes, never worn."** Some say he called it his best work. Others dismiss the anecdote as a literary folktale. Either way, the six-word story was born, and it's been popping around the writing world for years.

Launched online in 2006, SMITH Magazine celebrates personal storytelling and the ways in which technology has fueled storytelling's growth and infinite possibilities. We like to be both populist and aspirational, blurring the line between professional and amateur. So in November 2006, while thousands of people were cranking out tens of thousands of words during annual National Novel Writing Month, SMITH decided to lower the bar. We gave Hemingway's form a new, personal twist: What would a six-word memoir look like?

We asked our friends; they liked the idea. We ran it by memoirists we admire; they loved the challenge. We shared it with the tech communication wizards at Twitter.com; they wanted to team up to deliver a six-worder a day, free to anyone with a cell phone and a love of stories. With those pieces in place, we invited our readers to submit their short, short life stories for a contest—a battle of brevity.

Soon, six-word wonders were zipping across the Net—from laptops to SMITH, from Twitter to cell phones, from writers to their blogs, from readers to one another. And before we knew it, submissions were coming in by the thousands. Folks from all over the world sent in their sublime frustrations (**"One tooth, one cavity, life's cruel"**) and inspired aspirations (**"Business school? Bah! Pop music? Hurrah!"**), their divine wisdom (**"Savior complex makes for many** disappointments"), and deepest inner secrets (**"I like big butts, can't lie"**). And while most of the memoirs were penned by writers who have not been published (until now), others came from household names—from Aimee Mann (whose six is like a short, sweet song) to Mario Batali (who sent a generous half dozen to our table) to Joan Rivers (as outrageous and wonderful as you'd imagine).

We were most struck by the openness of the memoirists—and by their desire to share even more of their lives with perfect strangers. People sent us pictures of the adorable children they'd just admitted, in six words, they regretted having. One woman wrote us a letter detailing the infertility developments that had rendered her hopeful memoir obsolete. "Whole lifetimes happen in people's lives every day," she wrote, "so I suspect many memoirists write what's true at the time only to find their lives drastically different a short distance in the future."

The enthused author of **"Hockey is not just for boys"** sent in a photo essay of chicks with sticks, plus the skate-blade sharpening machine of which she's grown so fond. An artist in San Francisco followed up his book illustration with a comic strip about Anna Nicole Smith. We received photos of deceased wives in bridal gowns, of the tiny headstones of babies lost. An accountant in Florida requested a snail-mail address; soon a packet of miniature origami animals arrived at our office.

Others were rising to the occasion in ways we hadn't expected. We heard that teachers were assigning six-word memoirs to their students; that families were trading six-word memoirs across their dinner tables; that pet fanatics were writing them for their dogs.

We became as obsessed as our own memoirists. Wisdom started to appear everywhere in six-word increments. When a hand dryer in a public restroom bore the graffiti "love me or leave me alone," we took it as a six-word sign from above. We had whole conversations while counting on our fingers (and one thumb) for six-word legitimacy. We found ourselves debating the validity of hyphens over dinner and drinks. (Just how many words is "three-legged cat"?)

The fruit of this amazing response? You're holding it in your hands.

One of the delights of reading six-word memoirs is imagining the writer behind those few carefully chosen words. Despite the well-documented dangers of assumption, we were surprised to learn how many of the real-life writers were nothing like we expected.

The bittersweet **"Cursed with cancer. Blessed with friends"** came not from a wise, optimistic grandmother, but a nine-year-old thyroid-cancer survivor. The brave girl's mother wrote to say that her daughter had sat alone at the computer for hours selecting her words, and then checked SMITH each day, hoping to see her name on the screen. The poignant **"I still make coffee for two"** didn't come from the shaky hand of an elderly widower, but a recently dumped twenty-seven-year-old dude with a fondness for caffeine. After months of reading six-word memoirs barely noticing the writer's name, sometimes we were delighted by words seven and eight. After all, could you ask for a better life story from Deepak Chopra's son than **"Soul'd out so I could prophet"**?

This book is a glorious mishmash of these and myriad other voices; it's a thousand little windows into humanity—six words at a time. Whether the results are shocking, strange, silly, or sad, we hope you'll agree that they are always entertaining, often inspiring, and totally addictive.

The original edition of *Not Quite What I Was Planning* was published in February 2008. The book hit the *New York Times* bestseller list where, as fate would have it, it remained for *six* weeks. This deluxe edition has been revised and expanded to include more than sixty never-before-seen memoirs. We hope that you too will be swept away by the joy of six.

In the autobiographical spirit of SMITH Magazine, the photos and illustrations that appear here arrived from the writers themselves. To see hundreds of images we didn't have room for, plus new memoirs every day, go to **www.sixwordmemoir.com**. While you're there, you just might be struck by an overwhelming desire to supply a six-word memoir of your own. And why wouldn't you: Everyone has a story—what's yours?

The editors of SMITH Magazine
September 2007
New York, NY

Not
Quite
What I Was
Planning

After Harvard, had
baby with crackhead.

—Robin Templeton

Seventy years, few tears, hairy ears.

—Bill Querengesser

Watching quietly from
every door frame.

—Nicole Resseguie

Catholic school backfired.
Sin is in!

—Nikki Beland

Savior complex makes for
many disappointments.

—Alanna Schubach

Nobody cared, then they did.
Why?

—*Chuck Klosterman*

Some cross-eyed kid,
forgotten then found.

—*Diana Welch*

She said she was negative.
Damn.

—*Ryan McRae*

Born in the desert,
still thirsty.

—*Georgene Nunn*

A sake mom, not soccer mom.

—*Shawna Hausman*

I asked.

They answered.

I wrote.

—Sebastian Junger

No future, no past. Not lost.

—*Matt Brensilver*

Extremely responsible, secretly
longed for spontaneity.

—*Sabra Jennings*

```
Joined Army. Came out.
Got booted.
```

—*Johan Baumeister*

Almost a victim of my family.

—*Chuck Sangster*

The psychic said I'd be richer.

—*Elizabeth Bernstein*

Grumpy old soundman
needs love, too.

—*Lennie Rosengard*

Mom died, Dad screwed us over.

—*Lesley Kysely*

Painful nerd kid,
happy nerd adult.

—*L. J. Williamson*

Write about sex,
learn about love.

—*Martha Garvey*

Stole wife. Lost friends.
Now happy.

—*Po Bronson*

Fourteen years old,
story still untold.

—David Gidwani

One long train ride to darkness.

—Wayne Colodny

Wolf! She cried.
No one listened.

—May Lee

I'm my mother and I'm fine.

—K. Bertrand

All day I dream about sex.

—Guro Tupchileshtoff

I still make coffee for two.

−*Zak Nelson*

I like girls. Girls like boys.

—Andrea Dela Cruz

Never should have bought that ring.

—Paul Bellows

Sold belongings. Became Itinerant Poetry Librarian.

—Sara Wingate Gray

Tombstone won't say "had health insurance."

—Dean Haspiel

Stranded by ten-thousand-mile crush.

—Will Cockrell

Wasted time regretted
so life reinvented.

—Vicky Oppus

College was fun.
Damn student loans.

—Randy Boland

```
Semicolons;
I use them to excess.
```

—Iris Page

God chose. Said no. Now what?

—Adam Blackman

Time heals all wounds? Not quite.

—Jonathan Miles

Oldest of five. Four degrees. Broke.

—Kaitlin Walsh

Made a mess. Cleaned it up.

—Amy Anderson

A crush on Susan Sarandon.
Unrequited.

—Willy Edge

Says deaf boyfriend:
  you're too quiet.

—Anna Jane Grossman

Alive 38 years, feels like 83.

—Bryan Lowry

My family is overflowing with therapists.

—Shaina Feinberg

Boy, if I had a hammer.

—Tim Barkow

We still don't hear a single.

—Adam Schlesinger

Canada freezing. Gotham beckons. Hello, Si!

—Graydon Carter

`Years in the closet. Why? Why?`

—Michael Callahan

Docens liberos veritatem
vitam mihi docet.

—Michael Farmer

I did ask to live backwards.

—Helen Glynn

Forest peace, sharing vision,
always optimistic.

—Dr. Jane Goodall

Bespectacled, besneakered,
read and ran around.

—Rachel Fershleiser

Supported the sublime
with uncurbed
enthusiasm.

—Jeff Newelt

Followed white rabbit.
Became black sheep.

—Gabrielle Maconi

Middle of seven
made me me.

—Susan Sinnott

The woman formerly
known as Marissa.

—Mimi Ghez

Followed yellow brick road.
Disappointment ensued.

—Kelsey Ochs

Nerdy girl smutmonger.
Now, baby fever.

—Rachel Kramer Bussel

Born free, but lost my country.

–Ted O'Brien

Recent doctorate means overeducated and underemployed.

–Philip Sternberg

Taking a lifetime to grow up.

–Mirona Iliescu

Living for Jesus because
earth sucks.

–Johnny Johnson

Bad brakes discovered at high speed.

–Paul Schultz

Danced in
Fields
of Infinite
Possibilities.

—*Deepak Chopra*

Soul'd out so I could
prophet.

—*Gotham Chopra*

Strange name.
Transparent shame.
Instant fame.

—Bumble Ward

In the office. It smells here.

—Meera Parthasarathy

I am trying, in every regard.

—Lionel Shriver

Birth, childhood,
adolescence, adolescence,
adolescence, adolescence . . .

—Jim Gladstone

**Happiest when ignoring
huge financial debt.**

—Ayanna Bryan

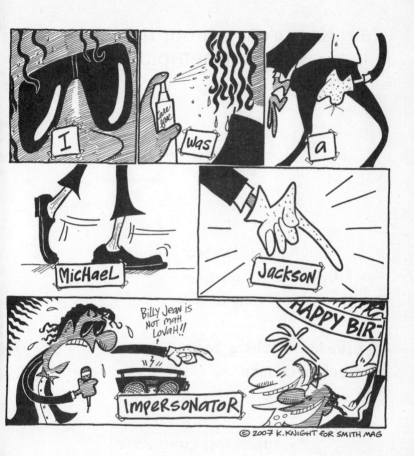

© 2007 K. KNIGHT FOR SMITH MAG

–Keith Knight

Not pretty enough
so now unemployed.

—*Stacey Smith*

I threw away my teddy
bear.

—*Margot Loren*

Mistakes were made,
but smarter now.

—*Christine Triano*

**Likes everything too
much to choose.**

—*Rachel Lindenthal*

Curly haired sad kid chose fun.

—*Stacy Abramson*

Now I blog and drink wine.

—Peter Bartlett

Egomaniac with inferiority complex defies odds.

—Lynne Vittorio

I thought I was someone else.

—Tysa Goodrich

Dancing for now,
one day farming.

—Eleanor Carpenter

Amazing grace: born naked,
clothed others.

—Mark Budman

Followed rules, not dreams. Never again.

—*Margaret Hellerstein*

My baby's name was Sydney Jane.

—*Margot Bertoni*

Love the men.
Hate the commitment.

—*Lindsay Filz*

I grew and grew and grew.

—*Randy Newcomer*

Starving artist.
Lucky break.
Life downhill.

—*Will Samson*

**Changing mind postponed
demise by decades.**

–Scott O'Neil

My spiritual path is 100 proof.

—John House

Wanted world,
   got world plus lupus.

—Liz Futrell

Yes to every date, met mate.

—Maria Dahvana Headley

The Hustle: turn champion
into sucker.

—Amarillo Slim

I was born
some assembly
required.

—Eric Jordan

I drank too much last night.

—*Meg McIntyre*

Study mathematics. Marry slut.
Sum bad.

—*Dan Robinson*

Took scenic route, got in late.

—*Will Blythe*

Raised Jehovah's Witness.
Excommunicated at 22.

—*Kyria Abrahams*

I like big butts,
can't lie.

—*Dave Russ*

I'm enjoying

downward

even this

dance.

—*Colum McCann*

Without ideas, intelligence could not exist!

—Ornette Coleman

I hope to outlive my regrets.

—Bob Logan

All night phone calls
complete me.

—Harry Manning

Tragic childhood can
lead to wisdom.

—Kristin Ahlemeier-Olfe

Sweet wife, good sons—
I'm rich.

—Roger Waggener

Barrister, barista,
what's the diff, Mom?

—Abigail Moorhouse

Mom, Dad. Daphne, Owen.
Who's next?

—Sean Wilsey

Which comes first:
tequila or accident?

—Penelope Whitney

Doing more for less is life.

—Rondell Conway

Cried. Defied, Denied. Sighed.
Died. Reapplied.

—Josh Gosfield

A sundress will solve
life's woes.

—*Kristen Grimm*

I recognize red flags
faster, now.

—*Barbara Burri*

I sucked even the lobster legs.

—*Rufus Griscom*

Anything's possible with
an extension cord.

—*billySIRR*

In and out of hot water.

—*Piper Kerman*

Life has gone to the dogs.

—*Ted Rheingold*

Moved to SF. Geek, not gay.

—Ryan King

Nothing profound,
I just sat around.

—Daniel Rosenburg

Found true love,
married someone
else.

—Bjorn Stromberg

Others left early: he
continued looking.

—Anthony Swofford

Shy Jersey kid,

overcompensating ever since.

—Ariel Kaminer

Dad died, mom crazy, me, too.

—Moby

```
Being a
monk stunk.
Better gay.
```

—Bob Redman

Quiet guy; please pay closer attention.

—Jonathan Lesser

Oklahoma girl meets world.
Regrets it.

—Gretchen Wahl

Life was but a dream,
merrily.

—Paul W. Morris

Happiness is a warm salami sandwich.

—*Stanley Bing*

Creative and destructive
in many ways.

—Meghan DeRoma

I sell hamburgers,
and french fries.

—Richard Maurer

Coffee junkie journalist
seeks trendy nerd.

—Jackie Olson

Fight. like. hell.
for. the. living.

—Susie Bright

On her birthday, my life
began.

—Lisa Parrack

Xenophile escapist tumbleweed globetrots, finds self.

—*Dominic Arizona Bonuccelli*

The shit invariably
hits the fan.

—Ashleea Nielsen

Blogging is easy.
Writing is hard.

—Jennifer Shreve

Quit Uni, have baby, now bored.

—Samantha Ng

I fell in love with Charlie.

—Kristine Allouchery

And he nerded
as never before.

—Jon Thysell

Iowa to Brooklyn,
    hair growing everywhere.

—William Johnson

Fix a toilet, get paid crap.

—Jennifer James

Tow truck drivers
are my psychiatrists.

—Joanne McNeil

Should have used
condom that time.

—Rob Bigelow

**Macular degeneration.
Didn't see that coming.**

—Ian Gould

Fifty years so far.
Happened fast.

—*Mark Michaelson*

Atheist plus Methodist make
Jewish children.

—*Richard Michelson*

Infinite calm beset with emotional
architecture.

—*DJ Spooky*

Won the fight;
lost the girl.

—*Jim O'Grady*

Near death experiences
are my forte.

—*Anna Mauser-Martinez*

Illustration by Josh Neufeld

Fight, work, persevere—
gain slight notoriety.

—*Harvey Pekar*

**Lived in moment
until moment sucked.**

—*Janine Goss*

She said nothing could go
wrong.

—*Derek Powazek*

Laughing until I pee my pants.

—*Carolyn Waller*

`Go find your father; my life.`

—*Adam Danielson*

Life goal:
Maximum results, minimal effort.

—*Phil Kahn*

Clawed my way out of Tennessee.

—*Nae Shell*

Quite undecided, yet hopefully
unsatisfied, generally.

—*Daniel Gumbiner*

Took a spectacle, made
it sport.

—*Dana White*

```
Slightly psychotic,
in a good way.
```

—*Patricia Neelty*

She walked barefoot
in wet cement.

—*Michelle Pinchev*

As a child, nomadic. Now static.

—*Kristin Gotski*

Mushrooms. Clowns. Wands. Five. Wig. Thatched.

—Amy Sedaris

Found true love after
nine months.

—Jody Smith

Hillbilly does right
by his teeth.

—Jason Snyder

No words can describe my life.

—John Baldridge

Afraid of everything.
Did it anyway.

—Ayse Erginer

On the playground, alone.
1970, today.

—Charles Warren

I wrote it all down somewhere.
—Ben Greenman

Inside suburban mom
    beats urban heart.
—Julie Goss

Missed Halley's Comet.
Miss virginity too.
—Yoz Grahame

Not a good Christian,
but trying.
—Alexander Tsai

Red diaper baby, hippie,
bourgeoise adult.
—Adrienne Ross

Lost and found, rescued by dog.

–Gail Reilly

Afraid of becoming like my mother.

–Jocelyn Pearce

Goodbye Fat Kim: I now live.

–Kim Kaufman

Two boys, my life,
conquering autism.

–Michelle DePasquale

Montana Jew—drives Toyota;
holsters pen.

–Michael Finkel

Mistakenly kills kitten. Fears anything delicate. —Susan Henderson

Illustration by Brian P. McEntee

What the hell.
Might as well.

—Nancy London

Hexed:
curse of the happy childhood.

—Cree McCree

Sometimes I'm crazy,
sometimes I'm sane.

—Bella Von Phul

Can't tonight,
watching *Law & Order.*

—Rory Evans

Musician gone bad.
Darn law school!

—Stephen Adams

I take photographs. I see life.

—*Daniel James*

Hippie parents.
Early independence.
Surprising success.

—*Darci Groves*

My life's a bunch of almosts.

—*Shari Bonnin*

Struggled with how
the mind works.

—*Steven Pinker*

It's not you. It's me. Honest.

—*Allison Glock*

Brought it to a boil, often.

—*Mario Batali*

Scribbling twit dreaming
lit every minute.

—Jamie Grove

Thought I would have
more impact.

—Kevin Clark

This is aggression in
pink, Mom.

—Nicole Tourtelot

Graduated May.
21 June.
Married July.

—Amara Rockar

Oh, to have just one puff!

—Suhana Selamat

Bad reputation,
  such a good girl.

—*Erin Oldroyd*

Mom left. Returned! Left.
Reconciliation! Cancer.

—*Kelly Streit*

Laughing intellectual
ronin danced,
unlearning lies.

—*Tom Buckner*

At the end of normal street.

—*Tracey Morgan*

Found great happiness in
insignificant details.

—*Alisdair McDiarmid*

Spent life looking
for dead people.

—Melody Lassalle

Forty Five.

Never Married.

Oh poo.

—Sonia Oney

Enjoying my fuck ups too much.

—Susan Crippin

My reach always
exceeds my grasp.

—Ray Garraud

Marked time till 55,
reborn thereafter.

—Doug Fraser

Details.
I really hate
drawing backgrounds.

—*Starline Hodge*

**Four children in four decades;
whew!**

—*Loretta Serrano*

An unusual turn of
gender circumstances.

—*Dragana Varadinac*

Hiding in apartment knitting
against depression.

—*Laurie White*

She kissed me and said yes!

—*Ricardo Saramago*

Dabbler in much, expert in none.

—*Joan Cady*

Once wed,
      twice loved,
           past prime.

—Betty Black

Grading AP essays,
I crave Tolstoy.

—Carinna Tarvin

Always dreamt of kissing pretty girls.

—Jessica Furey

I lost god. I found myself.

—Joe Kimmel

Everyone who loved me is dead.

—Ellen Fanning

circular. Caring for parents. life is

—*Timothy McGrath*

**It was embarrassing,
so don't ask.**

—Alex Lindquist

Verbal hemophilia.
Why can't I clot?

—Scott Mebus

Time to start over again,
again.

—Dan Petronelli

`Always even keel
except when sailing.`

—Maryann Pirrotta

Still lost on road less traveled.

—Joe Quesada

Over fifty, still a Boy Scout!

—Jerry Richstein

`The car accident`
`changed my life.`

—Kristin Stanefski

Said goodbye,
hasn't shut up since.

—Michael Collins

Burned my bridges and
my britches.

—Dave Zablocki

Trains, planes, thumb;
then children come.

—Karen Franklin

Older now, I draw myself better.

—*Peter Arkle*

Batteries are cheap.
Who needs men?

—Rebecca McLenna

Clueless meets Ophelia,
without the suicide.

—Larisa Ballinger

Atheist alcoholic gets
sober through God.

—Bob Todd

Discovered moral code
via Judy Blume.

—Beth Greivel

Artsy married Fartsy,
has two kids.

—Mary Organ

Anything possible—but I was tired.

—*Cheryl Family*

I ate, drank, and was hairy.

—*Yianni Varonis*

Girlfriend is pregnant, my husband said.

—*Shonna MacDonald*

I am awfully bored at work.

—*Chris Ponchak*

Learned reading, writing, forgot arithmetic.

—*Elizabeth Rose Gruner*

STILL HAVE NOT LEARNED TO SWIM

—Lauren Redniss

Trying to medicate my redneck past.

—*Garrett Sparks*

Lucky in love,
unlucky in metabolism.

—*Leah Weathersby*

I live the perfect
imperfect life.

—*Paul Lore*

Ate caterpillars.
Still won't grow up.

—*Chris Jackson*

Wannabe heroine but
just Plain Jane.

—*Tanya Holland*

Civil servant answers phone after five.

—*Jason Prince*

Glass half full;
pockets half empty.

—*Marina Guthrie*

We undercover agents
need mental toughness.

—*Joe Pistone*

Rebel librarian on
sabbatical from boys.

—*Heather Meagher*

Arthur-ectomy taking years!
Beware: wed cautiously.

—*Natalie Windsor*

Woman Seeks Men—
High Pain Threshold.

—Yin Shih

No Wife.
No Kids.
No Problems.

—Rip Riley

You are all in my imagination.

—Becky Weinberg

School geek married a
luscious cheerleader.

—Christopher Clukey

I couldn't protect me
from myself.

—Patrick Eleey

Eat mutate aura amateur auteur true.

—*Jonathan Lethem*

Aspiring lady pirate, disillusioned, sells boat.

—Diana White

Kentucky trash heap yields unexpected flower.

—John Kurtz

Married for money.
Divorced for love.

—Rosie Abraham

My life is a beautiful accident.

—J. D. Tenuta

Thank God I lived through Vietnam.

—Captain John Irving

Meat and potatoes man
goes vegetarian.

−Perette Lawrence

Smart, tall, independent woman.
Men scarce.

−Annie Schmidt

I was and now I'm not.

−Gayla Buyukas

Oh sweet nectar of life, coffee.

−Daniel Axenty

Young, skinny, ridiculed.
Old, skinny, envied.

−Phil Sweet

No shit I'm critical—
you're flawed.

—Elizabeth Koch

It's pretty high. You go first.

—Alan Eagle

One tooth,
one cavity,
life's cruel.

—John Bettencourt

In a Manolo world, I'm Keds.

—Colleen Cook

Lonely gay
hates work,
loves play.

—Ray Ivey

Wasn't noticed so
I painted trains.

—Mare 139

Chinese immigrant loathing drama
in Anaheim.

—*Eric Wong*

Running away:
best decision I made.

—*Stephen Elliott*

I served my debt to society.

—*Michael Frisch*

Scarred by 9/11;
helped by penguins.

—*Audrey Blackburn*

Fleeting nights, cloudy mornings,
coffee's ablution

—*Heath Hardin*

When she proposed, I said yes.

—Josh Neufeld

Black Latina. Slave ship stopped everywhere.

—Veronica Chambers

My heart is deaf, head dumb.

—David Matthews

My first concert: Zappa. Explains everything.

—Janet Tashjian

Nobody knows how I have suffered.

—Tim Hall

Dweeb, pussy . . . stronger than
anyone knows.

—Jim S.

**Wandering imagination
opens doors to paradise.**

—Rebecca Perlstein

**After eighteen years,
sold my book.**

—Susan Runholt

Too many lovers—
too little time.

—Joel Kincaid

Confused Communist child,
enlightened American engineer.

—Attila Kalamar

Couldn't cope so I wrote songs.

—Aimee Mann

Timid teacher takes
'tude from tykes.

—Kathy Gates

Angry guy gets law
license, sues.

—Bryan Gates

Long lost girl
recently found, unharmed.

—Tracy Bishop

Gave commencement address,
became sex columnist.

—Amy Sohn

3,000 miles away from
the truth.

—Michael Slenske

Mormon economist marries
feminist. Worlds collide.

—*Michael McBride*

Mormon feminist loves
husband, hates patriarchy.

—*Caroline Kline*

Followed dim shapes through narcotic haze.

—*John Law*

Mom, Dad have dementia. Got gun?

—*Carol Belding*

Born a twin, died a loner.

—*Heather Thompson*

```
Young optimist:
proven wrong.
Prematurely old.
```

—*Buzzy Porter*

It was worth it, I think.

—*Annette Laitinen*

Students laughed appreciatively. The
professor relaxed.

—Laurie Hensley

Drink because I am a poet.

—Maria Essig

People always pronounce
my name incorrectly.

—Linnea Jimison

Dorothy Gale had the
right idea.

—Pamela Vissing

Dropped out, got
out, lucked out.

—Ben Kweller

Take a left turn, then fly.

–Hillary Carlip

I was never the pretty one.

—Joan Nesbit Mabe

Born at 23,
childhood doesn't count.

—Krissy Karol

Perpetual work in
progress,
need editor.

—Sherry Fuqua-Gilson

Left Aruba for
Maryland.
Pretty dumb.

—Barbara Phillips-Seitz

I was the only planned
sibling.

—Mary Sebas

**Age grows,
I've finally accepted me.**

—*Kate Mammolito*

Paralyzed at fifty,
life still nifty.

—*Gib Henderson*

Snuggling, setups.
These are my specialties.

—*Laura Cooper*

Was big boy, now
little man.

—*Chris Cooper*

Lost Colorado wife.
Found Seattle life.

—*Jason Cain*

Ex-con making good
on lifestyle promise.

—Doug Houston

Canoe guide, only got lost once.

—Taylor Stump

**Aging late bloomer
yearns for do-over.**

—Sydney Zvara

American backbone,
Arab marrow,
much trouble.

—Rabih Alameddine

Memory was my drug of
choice.

—Pea Hicks

Liars, hysterectomy *didn't* improve sex life!

—*Joan Rivers*

Mom, sorry I moved to U.S.

—*Yuri Fukazawa*

Unhappy joke writer
hugs her chihuahua.

—*Jessica Salmonson*

Boys liked her.
She preferred
books.

—*Anneliese Cuttle*

Wife died young; on the mend.

—*Sumit Paul-Choudhury*

I'm ten, and have
an additude.

—*Tillie Seger*

**Gay physician designed
life-saving AIDS drugs.**

–Laurent Fischer

Never lived up to my potential.

–Leslie Sterling

Girl from Wisconsin
got to leave.

–Catherine Michalec

Tequila. Amnesia. Coincidence?
I think not.

–Larry Caraviello

Carbohydrates call my
name every day.

–Mary Petersdorf

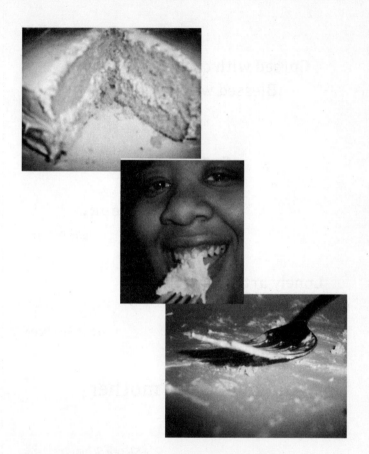

Never really finished
anything, except cake.

–Carletta Perkins

Cursed with cancer.
Blessed with friends.

—Hannah Davies

```
Crappy parents
killed
my self esteem.
```

—Julie Doherty

Lonely artist turned
waitress in love.

—Gretchen Bone

Does my biological mother
cry sometimes?

—Steven Schmidt

My life is just like yours.

—Matt Stephens

Some collect coins,
I collect diplomas.

—Srini Rajagopalan

Bipolar at 12, lithium at 36.

—Linda Hatfield-Southern

Navy dependent writes
American haiku poetry.

—Craig Jones

If Eliza Doolittle
wore cowboy boots . . .

—Dixie Friedman

Ex-wife and contractor
now have house.

—Drew Peck

Fifteen years since
last professional
haircut.

—Dave Eggers

Midlife crisis uncovers queer
intellectual's talent.

—*Donald W. Jacobson*

Fat jolly bearded origami-folding
accountant.

—*Gary Mullings*

Lucky in everything
else but love.

—*Eliot Sheridan*

Mixed blood.
I am America's future.

—*Holly Santiago*

I'm just here for the beer.

—*Alex Vournas*

With three cats
I'm never unloved.

—*Cynthia Macdonald*

Missing limb,
cruel world,
love overcomes.

—*James Mallon*

Divorced twice,
lived happily ever after.

—*Susan Guyaux*

Torrential tryst.
Terrible twins.
Tied tubes.

—*M. Brenner*

Can my words have
footnotes, please?

—*Amy Harbottle*

So it goes,
a tad askew.

—*Michael Dickter*

Alas, a farewell to legs. Next!

—*Allen Rucker*

Came, saw, conquered,
had second thoughts.

—*Harold Ramis*

`Left a desert for a`
`wasteland.`

—*James Slone*

City streets,
saggy shoes,
and poetry.

—*Arianna Kandell*

The weather is better up
here.

—*Brad Wieners*

Beat death thrice.
Still not religious.

—Shan Palmer

Found love.
Got hitched in Vegas.

—Jami Brandli

Baby dyke now raising
two babies.

—Andrea Selch

Stoned. Boned.
Where am I now?

—Sherry Levy

New Jersey to California.
Thank God.

—Ayelet Waldman

Town car,
    tailored suit,
        dirty nails.

—Nicole Blades

Bipolar secretary
    girlfriend mama hen
oddball.

—Teressa Fly

Learning to be great
at mediocrity.

—Christopher Reiger

**Jewfro and glasses,
laughter and yoga.**

—Deborah Greene

I fell far from the tree.

—Rebecca Stadolnik

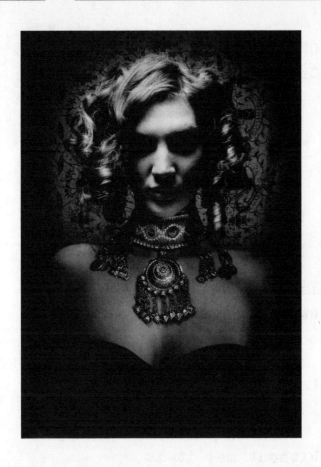

The image was large with silence.

—Elizabeth Raab

Chinese? American?
Chinese-American?
   The confusion endures.

—*Paul Chin*

After your jump,

the net appears.

—*Vincent Lauria*

Talkative female Trekkie
married male gamer.

—*Sarah Hairston*

I colored outside of the lines.

—*Jacob Thomas*

Without me, it is
just aweso.

—*Chris Madigan*

Me: consistently avoiding
   death since 1978!

—*Daniel Fowlkes*

I think, therefore I am bald.

—*Dickie Widjaja*

Should not have eaten
those mushrooms.

—*Emilie Raguso*

Wanked furiously.
Married. Furious no more.

—*John Heppolette*

Wealthy woman
escapes
with handsome
mailman.

—*April Shewan*

IBM brat broke back;
twins, Mac.

—John Hockenberry

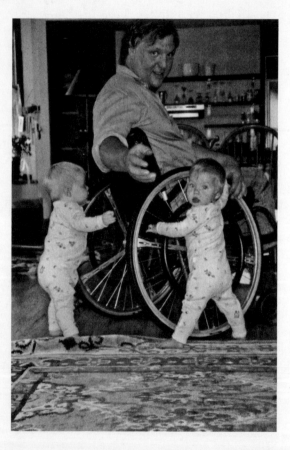

Love annihilated a
thirty-year age difference.

—*Betsy Smith*

Saw, interpreted, mourned,
hoped, then preached.

—*Douglas Rushkoff*

Even the quietest
sounds
make noise.

—*Paul Boggan*

I grew up in a cemetery.

—*Rachael Hanel*

Many hands have kept me afloat.

—*Nick Flynn*

Man of the world = alien immigrant.

—*Rajat Suri*

```
Ran away with
  circus; never
returned.
```

—*Ellia Bisker*

I managed not to
destroy anything.

—*Tucker Frazier*

All of my students hate me.

—*Sharon Fishfeld*

Gay white African
emigrates, finds love.

—*Graham Coppin*

ABCs
MTV
SATs
THC
IRA
NPR.

—Jancee Dunn

Buxom songstress loves love
and chocolate.

—Angie Arnold

Blade cuts,
blood runs,
scars remain.

—Heather Hudgins

Did I miss a deadline again?

—Bruce McGill

Walking the green mile:
finally free.

—Alejandro Echeverra

Redhead woman,
raucous curves,
makes music.

—Shannon Russell

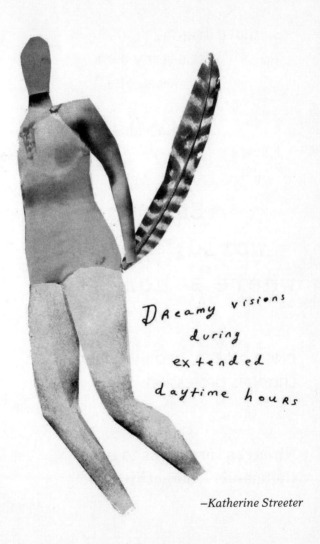

Dreamy visions
during
extended
daytime hours

—Katherine Streeter

Love drama,
just not my own.

—*Sam Zalutsky*

I wouldn't change it a bit.

—*Ann Paxton*

Saw the
world; now
where's home?

—*Hannah Silverstein*

Nose broken, beauty queen
changes profession.

—*Dan Rubin*

Nineteen forty-nine to two
thousand...something.

—*Anne Greer*

Blinked! Winked!
I am halfway through!

—Vinod Pillai

Arms: full. Life: not so much.

—Renee James

Quietly
cultivating my
inner Lynda Carter.

—Joanna Sheehan

Many risky mistakes,
very few regrets.

—Richard Schnedl

Six kids; life stranger than fiction!

—Deborah Carson

He left me for good eventually.

-*Audrie Lawrence*

Liberal at 18.
Conservative by 40.

-*Pat Ryan*

Would you like fries
with that?

-*Scott Northrup*

I won Miss Union
Pier 1952.

-*Elaine Yonover*

Legs spread,
I withheld my
intelligence.

-*Christine Granados*

Next time—

better parents, better hair.

—Ruth Romano

Little bit Lucy,
tempered by Ethel.

—Tami Maus

Traversing Earth together,
chasing elusive answers.

—Paul Barber

**Considered life, then death.
Step, repeat.**

—Paul Pope

Hockey is not just for boys.

—Alexandra Duplin

Artist, disabled.
Feeling mislabeled.
Ambitions tabled.

—Patrick Dentinger

Fell in love. Married.
Divorced. Repeat.

—Lori McLeese

Never liked the taste
of beets.

—Michael Pemberton

Underachieving
pleasure punk seeks
constant gratification.

—Dennis Elj

Always working on
the next chapter.

—Milan Pham

Business school? Bah!
Pop music? Hurrah!

—Max Robins

Happy now that I know myself.

—Anne Maiwald

Polka-dotted mayhem
and decadent disasters.

—Candace Locklear

Beach mama blissfully buoys
burgeoning brood.

—Elizabeth Barr

**Risked it all;
wasn't quite enough.**

—Greta Orris

I write because I can't
sleep.

—Ben Mezrich

Sperm too potent,
now have triplets.

—Renee Schunk

Never fear.
Truffle season is near.

—Barry Glassner

Yes, you can edit
this biography.

—Jimmy Wales

**The best hair, the worst
shpilkes.**

—Joanna Arkans

Katie180, you make
my heart crazy.

—John Patrick Zito

Started

small,

grew,

peaked,

shrunk,

vanished.

—*George Saunders*

**My daughter's baby,
inconvenient and incredible.**

—Laurie White

Mom blames musical theater.
I disagree.

—Dan Sigale

Insubordinate alien bookworm found
America, freedom.

—Katherine Scourtes

Big, little sister,
stuck in middle.

—Joanna Lilly

Short kid moves West;
climbs mountains.

—Mark Lilly

Multiple miscarriages.
Cousin will carry baby.

—*Joanna Brody*

Alone at home, cat on lap.

—*Christopher Goldthwaite*

Poet locked
in body
of contractor.

—*Marilyn Hencken*

And I never did sober up.

—*Ray Overfield*

Three marriages.
Thirteen novels.
Sleep's overrated.

—*Jane Heller*

World backpacking decade
ends with minivan.

—Cindi Hounton

Educated too much,
lived too little.

—Dan Vance

**Lapsed Catholic;
failed poet;
unpublished prayers.**

—Marc Sheehan

Twin girls,
double dates,
husbands confused.

—Naomi Beth Wakan

Went long on ride
toward Providence.

—Bill Buck

I imagined

more than

office jobs.

—*Gretchen Vitamvas*

Overjoyed I'm not like
my sister.

—Elizabeth DeLamater

Little German girl,
big American world.

—Lisa Turner

Hope my obituary spells
"debonair" correctly.

—Gregg Easterbrook

Just in:
boyfriend's gay.
Merry Christmas.

—Seshie Hargett

Traded mastheads for
Texas desert sky.

—Whitney Joiner

```
Lucky sperm club entrant
wins life.
```

—Steve Conlin

Was father, boys died,
still sad.

—Ronald Zalewski

Tried everything once,
few things twice.

—Ed Zevetski

Baptist Mom. Jewish Dad. Atheist.
Surprised?

—Sara Faith Alterman

**Cheated organizational
systems but never people.**

—Ryan Bright

Asked and
   answered,
   asshole,
   next question.

—*Joe Lockhart*

Really, doing fine,
thanks for asking.

—*Fuzzy Gerdes*

I'd rather be watching a movie.

—*Lawrence Levi*

Never could resist overachieving.

—*Chris Harris*

Her blue eyes
capture the distance.

—*Sonya Cheuse*

Born with glaucoma . . .
fading to black . . .

—*Susan Giusto*

I watched a lot of television.

—Adam Hirsch

```
Oh shit! No way? Yeah
  dude.
```

—Ned Vizzini

Girls from the Bronx are different.

—Arielle Basch

Five feet, but in
your face.

—Toby Berry

**Born bald. Grew hair.
Bald again.**

—A. J. Jacobs

Mistook streetlight for
the moon. Climbed.

–Zack Wentz

**Boyfriend in bed,
still a lesbian?**

–Cheryl Burke

I wrote a book about
this.

–Vittorio Giannini

```
Wanted to live forever,
died trying.
```

–Syona Luciferina

Hugged some trees,
then burned them.

–Tom Price

Happy child,
wild teenager,
adult anarchist.

−Dar Wolnik

Right place,
right time,
good lawyer.

−Ben Brown

To paraphrase William Faulkner: I endured.

−Don Willmott

To make a long story short . . .

−Jace Albao

Famished, I had
seconds . . .
and thirds.

−Richard Strager

Lazy Renaissance man
settles for dilettantism.

—Bradley Lyons

Raised a palimpsest,
by many voices.

—*Saba Cambone*

Arab hillbilly goes to New
York.

—*Alex Cummings*

Full life; impossible to
summarize in

—*Matt Love*

Was rebellious teen.
Now raising one.

—*Michelle Ganon*

I have not done it all.

—*Aaron Knoll*

Woke up,
fell down,
exited sideways.

—*Jim Clupper*

A new memoir every five years.

—*Srini Rajagopalan*

`My second grade teacher`
`was right.`

—*Janelle Brown*

Rather sing than stay to chat.

—*Keri Willson*

Someone had to pay the bills.

—*David Kuizenga*

Didn't fit in then;
   still don't.

—*Bob Fingerman*

I love my lady . . . and
bacon.

—*Jeff Walton*

Buried gold long ago.
Can't find.

—*Maureen Barnes*

Later-life serendipity
led to Authorland.

—*Jeff Schult*

A man, a plan, hot damn.

—*L. Levyne*

Revenge is living well,
without you.

—*Joyce Carol Oates*

I forgot I have memory loss.

–Mary Hynes

Underachieving . . . but willing to
overcompensate halfheartedly.

–Frank J. Lepiane

```
A Brooklyn lawyer.
Sewer to Sue-er.
```

–Mo Mann

Outcast.

Picked last.

Surprised them all.

–Rachel Pine

Country girl seeks,
finds, abandons city.

–Jenny Rose Ryan

What did you say? I'm deaf.

–*Karen Putz*

Became my mother.
Please shoot me.

–*Cynthia Kaplan*

Kinetosis, hemihypertrophy, testicular elephantiasis; pleasureboat recalcitrant.

–*Roderick Maclean*

Explained Hitler, Shakespeare.
Couldn't explain self.

–*Ron Rosenbaum*

If there's more,
I want it.

–*Alex Hart*

It's like forever,
only much shorter.

—Pete DeVito

God, grant me patience.
Right now.

—*Michael Castleman*

Cancer for sure. Still no cure.

—*Jenn Siebel*

Relatively famous parents,
very low self-esteem.

—*Molly Jong-Fast*

Pitched. Pitched. Pitched. Wrote.
Revised. Revised.

—*Andrew Adam Newman*

Lazy programmer,
ugly runner,
NASCAR dad.

—*Frank Gilroy*

Woman with man's name—
thanks, parents!

—Curtis Sittenfeld

Born lucky, striving to die
worthy.

—Julia Carpenter

**Tequila made her
clothes fall off.**

—Susanne Broderick

After Manson,
my life became dull.

—Allan Sorensen

I told you I was crazy.

—Michaline Babich

Topless dancer. Circus clown. Spy. Writer.

—Susan DiRende

Sometimes it rains.
Sometimes I smile.

—*Peter Hermann*

I play dress-up for a living.

—*Melissa Nicholl*

Where the hell are
my keys?

—*Brady Udall*

Bank robber,
prison-humbled,
confesses all.

—*Joe Loya*

Found transvestite
hooker. Travis is pleased.

—*Larry Tewksbury*

She always wore socks to bed.

—Myfanwy Collins

Not as blond as I look.

—Ellen Meister

Often alone,
office drone,
feisty crone.

—Patty Quickert

`Horny small-town boy`

`becomes writer.`

—Kevin Sampsell

I closely resemble
my uncle Fred.

—Brian Van Nieuwenhoven

Well, I thought
it was funny.

—*Stephen Colbert*

Strived to become
  everything I didn't.

—*Richard Tomas*

Let's just be friends,

she said.

—*Mike Pfaffroth*

Happenstance, she thought—
but maybe not.

—*Amelia Allard*

Chemistry? No. Law?
No. Motherhood? Yes!

—*Anneliese Dickman*

I died at an early age.

—*John Coyne*

Lived like no tomorrow;
tomorrow came.

—*C. C. Keiser*

Date with geek yields
chip-filled life.

—*Robin Raskin*

**I couldn't possibly
fuck him again.**

—*Theodore Bouloukos*

Learned everything from
words, pictures, love.

—*Dan Goldman*

This imperfect life,
perfect for perfectionist.

—*Sarah Gardner*

Forgot to say I love her.

—*Omi Castanar*

Can't read all the time.
Bummer.

—*Rina Bander*

I wrote a poem.
Nobody cared.

—*Joe Heaps Nelson*

Put whole self in, shook about.

—*Melissa Delzio*

Not quite what I was
planning...

—*Summer Grimes*

From Colombia to Columbia: 27 years.

—Marisa Catalina Casey

Mojo search resumes,
impossible flowers bloom.

-*Nick Balaban*

I inhale battles.
I exhale victories.

-*William Heath*

Working with what God gave me.

-*David Schmoyer*

Former band nerd
dreams big dreams.

-*Jesse Poe*

Coffee. Coffee.
Water. Water.
Wine. Tea.

-*C. Hunter*

Southern queer teacher
plays, sings, laughs.

—Amanda Northrup

Same Mistakes.
Over and over again.

—Matthew Oransky

Still trying
to impress my dad.

—Shoshana Berger

Hatless, shirtless,
shitless. Still, I sang.

—Scott Hartwich

Girl loved Jesus.
Girl loves boys.

—Lindsay Robertson

We were our own
Springer episode.
—*Michelle Hoogerwerf*

...exalted philanderer of the
English language...
—*Steven Ekstrom*

**Laughter and inappropriate
humor since 1985.**
—*Annie Jacobson*

I am a cartwheel of mentorship.
—*Anne Asher*

Asked for love.
Received confusion.
Waiting.
—*Irina Kendall*

I always suffered
fools fairly well.

—*Richard Ford*

I re-met Lori after 27 years.

–Alan Weinkrantz

So devastated, no babies for me.

–Jennifer Faulkner

Nobel dad; tough act to follow!

–Andreas Wettstein

Me: fully reformed and halfway happy.

–Koren Zailckas

Eat drink
man man
man man.

–Michael Musto

The day just kept getting better.

—Jeff Cranmer

Met lots of crazy famous people.

—Jonathan van Meter

Waited too long to get it.

—Rhona Yolkut

Took up photography.
Got the shot.

—Keith MacDonald

Strange like cat.
Smart like rat.

—Andrew Randall

I answer to the name Mom.

—*Lynne Chesterton*

Girls aren't 6'; I am 5'12.

—*Marlee Sayen*

Born in city that doesn't exist.

—*Jackie Delamatre*

Disco jeans, 1977: mine alone finally.

—*Susie Park*

Fact checker by day, liar by night.

—*Andy Young*

House of boarding passes,
like cards.

—Mike Kuniavsky

Weird quiet girl
fading from view.

—Felicia Sullivan

Four eyes are
better than
two.

—Marissa Walsh

Shot my penis in photo
booth.

—Jeffrey Zeldman

After which he was never sane.

—Aleksandar Hemon

**Gay Puerto Rican in
straight clothing.**

—Ryan Roman

Yes, singing rocks,
but money calls.

—Jonathan Cogswell

Almost nothing was
under my control.

—Joel Stein

Sold clocks carved out of
soap.

—Aaron Fagan

Learned. Forgot. Better
off relearning anyway.

—Brian DeLeeuw

More broken bones
than broken
hearts.

—Evan Rosler

Suburban girl tries
to make bad.

—*Sari Wilson*

Wife: one;
Degrees: two;
Arrests: seven.

—*Patrick J. Sauer*

Coulda, shoulda, woulda:
a regretful life.

—*Joe Maida*

These sails have never
settled long.

—*Justin Kownacki*

Let me in, you
narrative whore.

—*C. McClosky*

Fearlessness is the mother of reinvention.

—*Arianna Huffington*

It got better after middle age.

—Ruth Haworth

God who? Oh, him. No thanks.

—Carin Rhoden

Seeking route,
not sure of destination.

—Gary Belsky

Divorced! Thank God
for Internet personals.

—Maryrose Wood

Cheese is
the essence
of life.

—Mary Lynch

I waste time looking for love.

—*Sean Gannett*

Vietnam Protests.
Equality Protests.
Disability Protests.

—*Ron Kendricks*

My family did not
kill me.

—*David Sampliner*

Things happen because
I see holes.

—*Susan Chi*

Serial missed
connections
end with you.

—*Liz Brown-Inz*

Born in California.
Then nothing happened.

—*Mark Harris*

Named Hope. How else to be?

—Hope Hall

Straight jacket on
the gentle cycle.

—Stewart Rudy

Love Brooklyn,
but London still calls.

—Sarah Butterworth

Tickle, trample,
come back for more.

—Kathryn Waggener

I still secretly read
wedding magazines.

—Leslie Berryhill

Asian, white trash Scranton.
Let's Polka.

—Jeannie Lee

Eat to live, live to eat.

—Tim Toomey

The freaks, they
always find me.

—Ginger Lime

Wildly crooked,
unlikely to be straightened.

—lê thi diem thúy

Got a pony, broke my arm.

—Layne Bell

Should have learned
to count.

–*David Wheatley*

dam smart—
never lerned to
spel.

–*Rachel Ehrlich*

My ancestors were
accented cow herders.

—Nina Moog

Filled blank spaces with ambitious
endeavors.

—Adam Schachner

`Gin joints. Love affairs.`
`No relation.`

—Dean Ellis

I traveled each
and every highway.

—Sebastian Buhai

Widowed. Forging reluctantly
forward with faith.

—TerriAnn Ferren

Still a very bad
Mormon. Yay!

—Marsha Brown

This Tolstoy gets
no Oprah promotion.

—Victor Pelevin

Political stance makes
my family crazy.

—Steve Collins

Once was blind.
Now I see.

—David Hansen

Good things happen
to bad people.

—Michael Malice

Secret of life:

marry an Italian.

–Nora Ephron

Slightly flabby,
slightly fabulous,
trying hard.

—Amy Friedman

Palindromic novels fall
apart halfway through.

—Chuck Clark

Saw clearly after blind date. Marriage!

—Saralee Rosenberg

Thank god the suicide
attempt failed.

—Rhett Miller

Made labor-saving software: thousands
unemployed.

—George Girton

I hear nothing and see everyone.

—*Eunice Chang*

Secretly, I dream of
my ex-boyfriend.

—*Rosally Sapla*

Unfortunately,
there was no other way.

—*Atom Robinson*

A daydream, or so it seemed.

—*Eva Meszaros*

She danced, and
did little else.

—*Sarah Cost*

Came out.
Went in.
Came out.

—Earl Adams

Only black girl.
Fierce woman now.

—Courtney Kemp Agboh

My wife made me do it.

—Jeffrey Yamaguchi

Nature, nurture, lost, found, lost, found?

—Sarah Saffian

Other people's trash:
show and teller.

—Jason Bitner

birth
bris
bed
bath
and
beyond

—*Barry Blitt*

Like an angel. The fallen kind.

—Rick Bragg

Full of tequila and bad ideas.

—Buck Johnston

Lived in America.
Came back different.

—Nigel French

Lehmann-Haupt, yeah;
not that one.

—Rachel Lehmann-Haupt

Expected prime rib;
ended with hamburger.

—Bernard Lam

Drew on walls,
creative for life.

—DeAnna Sandoval

Unborn baby,
  dancing belly,
    arriving soon.

—Tami Piccione

Watchful crooked girl:
Comes with ink.

—Erin Cressida Wilson

Committed voluntarily,
until trying to leave.

—Michael Holland

When all else fails, start
running.

—Dean Karnazes

Carnivore and herbivore birth
magical omnivore.

—*Morgan Spurlock*

Never going to
have a dog.

—*Lily Redman*

Asked to quiet down; spoke
louder.

—*Wendy Lee*

My computer screen tells it all.

—*James Browne*

Indelibly tenacious,
I read and breed.

—*Shawna Lisk-Sprester*

Catholic girl. Jersey. It's all true.

—*Mary Elizabeth Williams*

Don't marry a lawyer, be one.

—Deborah Schneider

Still waiting for you to ask.

—Alice Massey

Ex-addict now addicted
to book deals.

—Susan Shapiro

When talk matters,
make it count.

—Phil Liggett

Love New York;
Hate Self. (Equally.)

—David Rakoff

My penultimate act is to imbibe.

—Alex Twersky

Mmm, tea.

So stereotypical.

Rule Britannia!

—Paul O'Brien

```
Arty dad, rocker mom,
crazy childhood.
```

—Summer Pierre

Ordering soup for two, for one.

—Dan Silverman

Still here despite
logic and likelihood.

—Elisha Marshall

She read too much . . .
into everything.

—Jessica Reed

Father, son, both hit by cars.

—Gordon Hurd

Women's magazine
employee now
misogynist novelist.

—Stephanie Lessing

I didn't skateboard
nearly often enough.

—Kevin Wilkins

Internet famous,
for what that's worth.

—Ron Hogan

Sometimes at night I lay lonely.

—Mark Jaynes

**Deported once,
legal now—Green Card.**

—Michael Kaminer

I didn't walk off a roof.

—Tobin Levy

```
Say no now, I
now know.
```

—Steve Woodruff

Left house one day
for cigarettes.

—Sheila Ryan

What?
Lemony Snicket?
Lemony Snicket?
What?

—Daniel Handler

Made some good choices,
   got lucky.

—*Matthew Kett*

```
Jew-born.
Yeshiva-educated.
Date goyim.
```
—*Abby Ellin*

Pop split; I write him in.

—*Sepideh Saremi*

True love was prevented
   by leprosy.

—*Peter Hayward*

Pay attention to

me! Go away.

—*Kathy Rogers*

Big hair, big heart, big hurry.

—Larry Smith

Melancholy marvel at how
everything connects.

—Lawrence Weschler

Climbing, porn, crack,
science. Still bored.

—Lenny Oliker

I'm the fine print;
read closely.

—Kristina Grish

Ran east, ran west, ran late.

—Susie Smith

```
Will draw for
food and coffee.
```

—*Molly Crabapple*

Most Turkish Kurd, most
Kurdish Turk.

—*Yasar Kemal*

Tall, dark, handsome:
Single, content, uncommunicative.

—*Mark Grace*

```
Do as say, not as did.
```

—*Emily Gordon*

Good, evil use the same font.

—*Arthur Harris*

Detergent girl:
Bold. Tide. Cheer. All.

—*Martha Clarkson*

Never a bridesmaid;
always a bride.

—*Anne Allisoni*

I fell out of the
nest.

—*Jason Logan*

More than yesterday,
less than tomorrow.

—*Nichiren Nahuel Palombo*

I don't nibble. I bite.
Hard.

—*Matthew Torres*

Open road, no map.
Great Scenery.

—*Tom Gabbay*

Maybe you had to be there.

—*Roy Blount Jr.*

Right brain working
left brain job.

—*Dave Terry*

Life behind a
microphone
gets lonely.

—*Crystal Kash*

Spent longing for
the seventh word.

—*Ron Bel Bruno*

Five continents down; two to go.

—*Virginia Graham*

Affection. Erection.
No protection.
Injection. Infection.

—*Colleen Zachary*

Speaks mind especially when losing it.

—Ellis Reid

He knew her bruises would fade.

—Colin Stanton

Indeterminate.
Not enough data for conclusion.

—Ian Grant

Tunneling underground, lured
deep by ghosts.

—Danielle Trussoni

I got herpes, in my pants.

—Daniel Moyer

Veni, vidi,
but haven't vici yet.

—Meenakshi Nandini

Hid for a while. Not anymore.

—*Ginger Voight*

I came, I saw, I concurred.

—*Cris Anitsirhc*

Afraid of mirrors,
too many marshmallows.

—*Lihi Lasslo*

Bought American Dream.
More like nightmare.

—*Harry McCoy*

I was concerned
about my obituary.

—*James Dunn*

Born red closet reborn SF queer.

—David Boyer

Youngest of four girls
turns fifty.

—Judi Kolenda

Saw the sky and
started walking.

—Mark Sundeen

Learned eventually,
Billy Crystal, not Salinger.

—Ben Kaplan

Once born,
now old,
soon gone.

—Andre Vandal

We were married in the snow.

–Polly and Andrew McLean

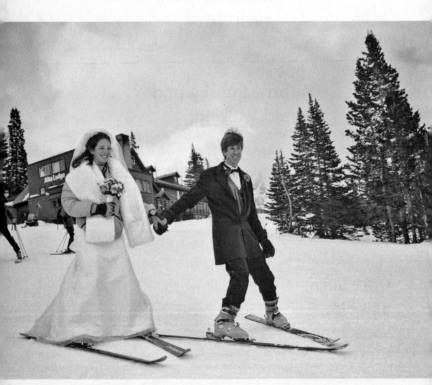

Photograph by Sean Graff

My life, in Mexico, is strange.

—*Cosima Rose*

Awkward girl takes chances.
Fun ensues.

—*Charlotte Riley*

The light that night was perfect.

—*Lara Swimmer*

Better living through chemistry,
sans love.

—*Greg Rainwater*

I auditioned.
I got the
part.

—*Faith Hoffman*

Entire story written
with quotidian nouns.

—*Tim Batton*

Losing your identity can be
fearsome.

—*Robyn Crawford*

Giraffe born to a farm family.

—*Grant Langston*

Lived life,
playing metal,
went deaf.

—*M. Kincaid*

I write stories. They come true.

—*Rebecca Woolf*

Struggling Southern eccentric finding my happiness.

—*Leigh Ann Apanites*

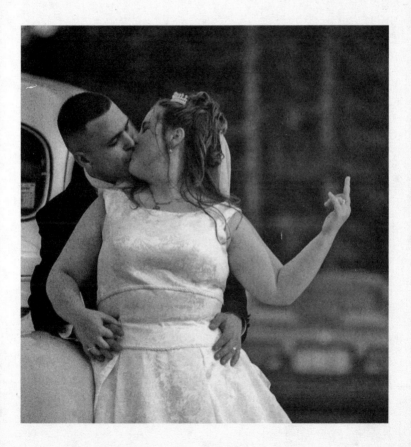

Act two curtain brought
dramatic improvements.

—*John Godfrey*

Saw a glimpse,
should have risked.

—*Lori Flaherty*

Hey Red, order up! Chop! Chop!

—*Patty Griffin*

Somehow, she lived
without an iPod.

—*Jennifer Crouser*

Last words,
our daughter,
too soon.

—*Steve Allen*

Killed. Loved.
Got high on everything.

—*David Booth*

Lonely, frothy kisses,
then only spite.

—*Stephania Serena*

Dead mom watching. I'll be good.

—*Israel Hyman*

Became more like myself
every year.

—*Eddie Sulimirski*

Rich in degrees
and student loans.

—*Barb Piper*

He was happy being a flasher.

—Fred Telegdy

Old and married.
Hot classmates. Sigh.

—Bill Johnson

Nerdy, wordy,
learned to shut up.

—Caren Lissner

```
Type A personality.
Type B capability.
```

—Keith Lang

High school dropout
but college graduate.

—Mary Beth Nalin

Dreamed of endless love.
Awoke alone.

—Mohammad Fatayerji

Adolescence, internet,
internet, internet, internet,
death.

—Josh Rosenfield

We were each other's
favorite person.

—Montana diLemonada

Surname rhymes with
profanity.
Childhood torture.

—Noah Smit

Must remember: people,
gadgets. That order.

—Brian Lam

Learned to live with great loss.

—*Michele Wytko*

Sex overrated.
Went and got castrated.

—*Alex Warren*

Occassionally wrong but
never in doubt.

—*Layne Butler*

Illiterate poet saw
far too much.

—*Robert Strassburg*

WASP wants
to be soul
man.

—*Scott Pratt*

Me see world!
Me write stories!

—Elizabeth Gilbert

Alabama boy said hallalujah,
wrote memoirs.

—*Paul Thornton*

Normal female blogs
for a living.

—*Sarah Weinman*

Accidents cause people—
son is wonderful.

—*Laurie Reinhart*

Impoverished black male.
Harvard Law bound.

—*Robert Young*

Leaving:
I toss blame like grenades.

—*Tanya Jarrett*

Born ready, bad eyes and all.

—Hua Hsu

Thought long and hard.
Got migraine.

—Lisa Levy

Ten strikes against me,
hit homerun.

—Maxine Jennings

Despite disorders, jafroed
jewboy gets girl.

—Michael Eisner

Older orphan,
creates family with friends.

—Theresa Neinas

That Kiss song says it all.

—*James Hampton*

I can resist everything
except temptation.

—*Carolina Conte*

Should have risked

asking, he sighed.

—*Gino Serdena*

Here: Macaca! There: American!
Where, beloved?

—*Mitali Perkins*

Never should've done that first line.

—*Joshua MacPhetridge*

Adopted?
Are you fucking
shitting me?

—Darius Logan

Traveling the road,
    writing science fiction.

–*Henry Melton*

Hard to write poems
from prison.

–*Ellen Goldstein*

Born in abject obscurity;
never escaped.

–*James Blum*

Friends all Jewish.

I'm merely neurotic.

–*Brian Mahon*

Suburban Christian child.
Hippie agnostic adult.

–*Shannon Barnes*

Writing and drawing
brought me here.

—*Gabrielle Bell*

Alaskan hippie kid. Escaped via Ph.D.

—*Melanie Brewer*

Clumsy girl found adventure. Also, bruises.

—*Rebecca Campbell*

Jury believed me; prison awaits him.

—*Jessica Yu*

Realized childhood dream doesn't pay bills.

—*Nicole Williams*

Mostly waited for the big stuff.

—*Jennifer Smith*

Taught lies.
Discovered truth.
Neither matters.

—Gautham Nagesh

**Born into a life
worth living.**

—Cher Tushiah

Met Jesus early, then ran fast.

—Jessica Thompson

I'm not afraid of
anything anymore.

—Kathryn Hammond

The road diverged; I took it.

—Rachel Farris

Eight thousand orgasms.

Only one baby.

—Neal Pollack

Loved a man, then a woman.

—*Kate Evans*

Product of obscure
American colonial
ancestors.

—*Randy Seaver*

Brainy widowed sexpot
raises hell, kids.

—*Jennifer Johnson*

Wounded girl turns life into
stories.

—*Farai Chideya*

The militant who became a monk.

—*Mike Adams*

Born in Baghdad, I said enough.

—Shwan Taha

Most successful accomplishments
based on spite.

—Scott Birch

Haunting dad,
spotlight mom,
retrieving marriage.

—Nell Casey

She left Texas none too soon.

—Jen Worrell

Carries flask for
unsociable social events.

—Janina Williams

He wore dresses.
This caused messes.

—Josh Kilmer-Purcell

Man, slightly disgruntled,
may throw poo.

—Egan Fowler

It's all about me, isn't it?

—Daniel Halpern

My memoir? You can't be serious.

—Dan Menaker

EDITOR. Get it?

—Kate Hamill

I always took the
joke too far.

—Thomas Hamill

Big nose, British chicken legs:
beautiful!

—*Jen Gabel*

I will never be
quite finished.

—*J. P. Hoban*

Learning disability, MIT.
Never give up.

—*Joe Keselman*

Glory developing vital loving
fighting life.

—*Josh Lucas*

Just a rockin' readin'
knittin' kitten.

—*Emmeline Friedman*

Looking to know everything
about everything.

—Tor Andersen

Philosophical teen,
surrounded but sometimes lonely.

—Nehemiah Blazek

Retired music teacher
enjoys life's symphonies.

—Caroline Baker

Liked by all. Known by
few.

—Zell Williams

Age eleven:
became a middle
child.

—Matt Farrell

Dad wore leather pants in Reno.

–John Falk

Illustration by Bob Salpeter

Worse fates have befallen better men.

—Stanley Morgenstern

18 years old,
first kiss uncertainty.

—Jerrica Moore

Polio gave me my happy life.

—Ruth Thompson

Big heart protected
by sharp tongue.

—Kris Kleindienst

```
I tried. It was not
enough.
```

—Robert McCarty

Learned to say no too late.

—Jonathan Engle

There will be no
beautiful corpse.

—Sharon Lewis

You must be fifty to
understand.

—Rev. Henri Breitenkam

Loved God, reason,
   simplicity; authored
   books.

—Patricia Williams

He always liked to live
fast.

—Jesse Burkett

Former child star
seeks love, employment.

—*Justin D. Taylor*

Didn't pull out.
Downhill from there.

—*Roger Daubach*

Fears commitment, debt.
Attracts spouse, house.

—*Beth Grundvig*

Rubber nipples,
dimpled thumbs,
Camel Lights.

—*Dawn Ryan*

Smart, humble, shy.
Notice me, please?

—*Ryan Kucera*

Wasn't born a redhead;
fixed that.

—Andie Grace

Found a demon to love forever.

—Aaron Olson

Made costly mistakes,
learned valuable lessons.

—Ricky Roach

Green eyes,
freckled skin,
waiting womb.

—Heather Thompson

Naively expected logical world.
Acted foolish.

—Emily Thieler

Partied a ton,
then had kids.

—*Paul Tullis*

Don't I know you
from college?

—*Jean Chatzky*

Cadavers played an
unexpectedly large part.

—*Mary Roach*

Sexy single; married
not so much.

—*Vicki Botnick*

New Yorker: everything
pisses me off.

—*Russel Fershleiser*

Battled the bulge, became food critic.

—*Anthony Giglio*

Climbed mountains.
Didn't like the view.

—*Sarah Morrow*

Used to add.
Now I subtract.

—*Melissa Gorelick*

Tried not believing
everything I thought.

—*Beth Linas*

Loved home.
Left to make sure.

—*Adam Krefman*

Fifth grade project:
Dressed as Pope.

—*Sarah Wise*

Surrounded by beauty in all forms.

—*Jennifer Pliego*

Showed up sober, often left otherwise.

—*Amber Kitzler*

Loved Natalie,
loved Jacqueline,
married Debbie.

—*Joe Barker*

I stay still,
chaos finds me.

—*Jennifer Rutherford*

Internal age doesn't match external age.

—*Carol Smith*

Grew up quiet,
learned to yell.

—*Ana Cruz*

Former miserable queer
turned strangely gay.

—*James Barry*

Sometimes six is five too many.

—*Sean Marier*

Seeds,
flowers,
pollen,
bees,
honey,
toast.

—*Jeanette Cheezum*

This page was intentionally left blank.

—Tai Moses

Live,
then write; live again,
    repeat.

—Lauren Gonzalez

Around the world in 80 guys.

—KC Sanders

Despite best efforts,
didn't die young.

—Donald Miller

Rabbit-punched, horse-whipped,
hen-pecked, dog-tired,
but uncowed.

—Anthony Gordon

He wanted much;
he feared more.

—Randall Currey

Love my kids, adore my horses.
—*Dagne Tremblay*

Death, divorce,
heartbreak, cancer.
Chocolate helped.
—*Linda Farbstein*

Been there, done
that, loved it.
—*Sid Singh*

Memories of kissing … your name
again?
—*Regina Villegas*

Any greenhorn
can garden in Iowa.
—*Genie Gratto*

Teacher sits cross-legged with her
children.

−*Susan Louis*

Living in sin
through female lips.

−*Laura Ruiz*

Katrina and **Obama**
motivate me equally.

−*Errol Bullock*

Everything intangible piled
higher and deeper.

−*Thomas Vance*

You cheated, but it's my fault?

−*Sheila Bacon*

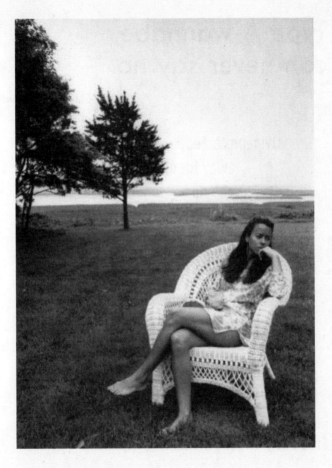

I photoshop people in my head.

–Abigail Pope

Type A wannabe,
can never say no.

—Meaghan O'Neill

Over-protected,
away for college,
drug problem.

—Daniel Armstong

Survived by his wife and children.

—Matt Sickles

Jewish American princess
brilliantly hocks bibles.

—Stefanie Lindner

In every footfall I am complete.

— Cindy Lauwasser

Loved by all but her lovers.

—*Jesika Becker*

Rube out of West.

Still lost.

—*Anthony Ramirez*

Neither lender nor gender bender be.

—*Kat Herding*

`Chef extraordinaire,`
`timing off, cooking on.`

—*Connie Dingle*

Send to all . . .
   No, wait! Shit.

—*Robert Dempsey*

What
they
see
in my
eyes.

—*Johan Santana*

Dog and guitar,
guide and company.

—David Rusty Perez

Lost ten years to Daddy problems.

—Bella Von Phul

*Traded my keyboard for a
pincushion.*

—Molly Ditmore

Have teenage son,
I need drugs.

—Kim Ramage

Emotional wreck with sense of humor.

—Jacqueline Levine

Lost reality, but became a cybernaut.

—*Dejan Milenkovic*

I've lived in terror
of myself.

—*Mark Wagener-Perkins*

Wife has cats.
Husband's clothes furry.

—*Lawrence Hernandez*

Rolling
   down
      a hill
         with sisters.

—*Adrian Lansdown*

No thank you, I'm just looking.

—*Kariann Burleson*

Dad dreams different mousetrap.
Oops.
Again.

—Jacob Reider

Surrounded by girls,
birthed boys,
bewildered.

—Nancy Friedman

Quiet, controlled chaos, can it be?

—Andre Kerman

Fried chicken.
Mayonnaise.
Hot sauce.   RIP.

—Joe Yang

My dears, I miss you so.

—Barbara Ascher

They attacked, we survived;
let's eat.

—*Charles Hollander*

Loser geek climbs social corporate ladder.

—*Tony Leach*

`Old creaseless face,`
`cold passionless soul.`

—*Seraphie St. Claire*

Sold Rolls Royces.
Had no choices.

—*Linda Stromme*

Dream girl me,
oh yeah, right.

—*Katie Bowen*

Last child flees suburbs, balls out.

—*Michele Arboit*

Will die with my boots on!

—*Alan White*

Saved by women's magazines.
How Bazaar.

—*Cathy Alter*

Left in landslide's dust,
soy asi.

—*Chad Swimmer*

No, you are in MY way.

—*Mark Korchinski*

I thought I would be taller.

—Lisa Brown

Tell your story.
That's my story.

—Andy Goodman

These words are
yours to keep.

—Alec Ounsworth

On the seventh
word, he rested.

—Stephen J. Dubner

Index